WHISKEY

PASSPORT

Drams From Around The World

NAME:
ADDRESS:
NEXT OF KIN:
LOCATION OF WILL:

**PASTE / DRAW
YOUR PHOTO
HERE**

CREATED BY HOLLY L. LÖRINCZ
MACGREGOR'S WHISKEY BAR
MANZANITA, OREGON

How To Use Your Passport

Use this journal as a reference tool for your future bar or distillery visits. Or, when you have managed to fill these pages with whiskies from around the world, brag loudly to the person on the stool next to you, then drink a lot of water and call for a ride home. Journaling guidelines:

1. Choose a brown liquor.
2. Drink a dram and sigh in delight.
3. Shut one eye and read the label. Don't be ashamed if you need to ask the bartender for reading glasses from the lost and found.
4. Record the name, type of whiskey, and date under the appropriate region or country. Write in the age and proof. Be sure to add a description of the flavor and, on a scale of 1 to 5, if you'd order it again. For example, if you order a rye, you could flip to the rye page and write something like this:

Angel's Envy Rye
7 yr, 100 proof
Tried this at MacGregor's Whiskey Bar, October 2017.
Made in Kentucky. Distilled in rum barrels and
tastes like caramel. Best rye, ever.
A 5+. Must find a bottle.

Table of Contents

A Few Terms to Get You Started

UISGE BEATHA The "water of life," in Gaelic. *Uisge* is pronounced Wh-sh-kah, giving us today's word for whiskey.

SCOTCH WHISKY Any whisky distilled and aged at least three years in Scotland, and containing at least some malted barley, is a scotch. Much of the scotch whisky (no "e" if it's from Scotland) from the south is peaty, but northern labels are not nearly as smoky.

IRISH WHISKEY (Note the "e") A lighter, sweeter whiskey, almost always blended, and produced in Ireland.

AMERICAN WHISKEY Whiskey that is made in America from a minimum of 51% malted barley (though this definition is sometimes disputed, claiming rather that American just means made in America).

BOURBON Whiskey made from a minimum 51% corn.

RYE Whiskey made from a minimum of 51% rye.

RUM Another brown liquor, rum is distilled sugarcane.

SINGLE MALT A whiskey using only a single grain, A malt whiskey must contain only malted barley and water. Fun fact: Scottish malt whisky must be made in a pot still.

BLEND Duh. Whiskey made from a blend of cereal grains, or from a blend of other whiskies. Chivas Regal, Dewar's, Johnnie Walker are blended scotch whiskies.

SMALL BATCH WHISKEY This is when select barrels of whiskey have been used to create a blend that matures into a specific style.

PEAT This is a very old, compressed layer of grasses, roots, plants, and moss commonly found in Scotland and Ireland, often used as a heat source like coal. Whiskey makers from Scotland will use it to dry malted barley. It is the peat smoke that flavors the scotch.

MASH The mixture of cooked grains and water that gets mashed up before the fermenting yeast is added.

DISTILL Distilling means taking your mash that has had the yeast added—and so is fermenting—and placing that in a still, where it will be heated. The heat vaporizes the alcohol, which is caught, turned back to liquid, and stored. Water is added to lower the proof.

POT STILL This type of still, made of a large copper pot, is most commonly used to produce single malt whiskies.

COLUMN STILL Also known as a continuous or Coffey still, this still has tall copper columns, pouring a continuous stream of liquid over steam-producing plates.

CASK After the mash of grain is distilled, the resulting liquid is usually placed in either American White Oak or European Oak cask barrels. The type of wood and treatment affect the taste, obviously. For example, bourbon casks are charred on the inside. The liquid that evaporates over time is called the "Angel's Share."

AGE Whiskey becomes more flavorful and complex the longer it ages. The year on the bottle tells you the age of the youngest whiskey in the blend.

PROOF The proof, or strength, is the Alcohol Per Volume (ABV). A 100% proof means the liquor is 50%

alcohol. Pay attention to this if you're settled in for a long night of sampling. Stick with a lower proof, unless you've got the liver of a Scot or an Irishman.

DRAM When you order a glass of sipping whiskey, you're ordering a dram. Ask for a "Wee dram o' your finest," bartenders love that.

NEAT Order your sipping whiskey neat in order to be served a single, unmixed liquor at room temperature. If you don't want ice, say "up." Many serious whiskey drinkers order their dram neat, up, with a side of water. Adding a drop or two of water (using a straw or dropper) to the whiskey in your glass can open up the flavors.

NOSE The aroma of a whiskey is called the nose. Go on, stick your nose right on into that glass and breath deep. Most experts will tell you there are three parts to drinking whiskey: Eyeing it, which is checking out the color and thickness; Nosing it, which is smelling for flavor distinctions; and Tasting it, which means noticing the initial taste and the finish.

Scotch Whisky

SPEYSIDE REGION
The most popular scotch region on the island, known for its sweet and smooth scotches. Some of the most well known are: the Macallan, the Glenlivet, and Glenfiddich.

Scotch Whisky

HIGHLANDS REGION
Known for its high quality and wide variety of tastes. Some of the most popular are: Glenmorangie, Dalwhinnie, Oban, or Clynelish

Scotch Whisky

ISLAY REGION
Pronounced Eye-luh, this region is known for its smoky, peaty scotches. Examples: Laphroaig, Lagavulin, and Ardbeg

Scotch Whisky

LOWLANDS REGION
Known for its lighter scotches, the biggest variety, and is
the fastest growing region. Some of the most popular are:
Glenkinchie, Auchentoshan, and Bladnoch.

Scotch Whisky

ISLANDS REGION
Far fewer scotch whiskies, but known for being full flavored. Some of the most popular are: Highland Park, Talisker, and Jura

Scotch Whisky

CAMPBELTOWN REGION

The smallest of the scotch regions, there are only a handful of remaining distilleries. Some of the most popular are: Springbank, Glen Scotia, and Kilkerran.

Scotch Whisky

BLENDED SCOTCH WHISKY

While not a region, obviously, many of the country's most popular scotch whiskies are blends of various distilleries. Some of the most well known are: Johnnie Walker, Dewar's, Chivas Regal.

Irish Whiskey

Examples: Jameson, Redbreast, Bushmills, Tullamore Dew

American Whiskey

Examples: McCormick Special Reserve, D. Nicholson 1843, Kentucky Gentleman

Bourbon

KENTUCKY
Examples: Knob Creek, Old Grand Dad, Maker's Mark

Bourbon

TENNESSEE
Examples: Jack Daniel's, George Dickel, Chattanooga

Bourbon

ANYWHERE ELSE
Examples: Virginia Gentleman, Breckenridge, Rand and
Spear Bourbon Whiskey

Rye

Examples: Angel's Envy Rye, Knob Creek, Van Winkle Family Reserve, Wild Turkey Rye, Whistlepig

Oregon Whiskey
(Because Oregon has damn fine whiskey)

Examples: McCarthy's Oregon Single Malt Whiskey, House Spirit's Westward Oregon Straight Malt Whiskey, Big Bottom Barlow Trail Blended Whiskey, Bull Run's Temperance Trader Straight Bourbon Whiskey, and Pendleton Whisky (blended in Canada, distilled in Oregon)

Canadian Whiskey

Examples: Crown Royal, Forty Creek, Hiram Walker

Japanese Whiskey

Examples: Hibiki 12 Year, Nikka Pure Malt Whisky 12 Year, Suntory, Single Malt Yoichi, Fuji Gotemba

Australian Whisky

Examples: Cradle Mountain, Black Gate, Old Hobart

Rum

CARIBBEAN
Examples: Appleton Estate 21 Year Old Rum, El Dorado 12 Year, Bacardi 8 Year, Havana Club, Cruzan Rum

Rum

UNITED STATES
Examples: Cannon Beach Distillery Rum, Balcones Texas Rum, Old Ipswich Rum, Three Sheets Rum, Deep Island Hawaiian Rum

Rum

ANYWHERE ELSE
Examples: Santa Teresa 1796 Ron Antiguo Solera from
Venezuala, Bundaberg Rum from Australia, Cana Brava
from Panama, Flor de Caña 7-Year-Old Grand Reserve
from Nicaragua

More Countries or Regions

The following countries have established distilleries; feel free to add to the list.

DOMINICAN WHISKEY

ENGLISH WHISKEY

FINNISH WHISKEY

FRENCH WHISKEY

GERMAN WHISKEY

INDIAN WHISKEY

NEW ZEALAND WHISKEY

SOUTH AFRICAN WHISKEY

SWEDISH WHISKEY

WHISKEY PASSPORT: DRAMS FROM AROUND THE WORLD

By Holly L. Lörincz
MacGregor's Whiskey Bar, Manzanita, Oregon

Benchmark Press Publishing
Copyright © 2017

ISBN-10:
0-9961192-4-8
ISBN-13:
978-0-9961192-4-5

Printed in the United States of America
Cover Photo Credit: Breanna Stephens

www.ingramcontent.com/pod-product-compliance
Lightning Source LLC
Chambersburg PA
CBHW021337290326
41933CB00038B/955